MW01106035

GIANTS OF THE OLD TESTAMENT

LESSONS ON LIVING FROM
JOB

A devotional by
WOODROW KROLL

BACK TO THE BIBLE
Publishing

JOB
published by Back to the Bible Publishing
©1999 by Woodrow Kroll

International Standard Book Number
0-8474-0693-8

Edited by Rachel Derowitsch
Cover design by Robert Greuter
& Associates

All Scripture is taken from
the New King James Version.
Copyright © 1979, 1980, 1982,
Thomas Nelson, Inc.
Used by permission.

ALL RIGHTS RESERVED
No part of this publication may be repro-
duced, stored in a retrieval system or
transmitted, in any form or by any
means—electronic, mechanical photo-
copying, recording or otherwise—except
for brief quotations in printed reviews or
articles, without the prior written permission of the publisher.

For information:
BACK TO THE BIBLE
POST OFFICE BOX 82808
LINCOLN, NEBRASKA 68501

1 2 3 4 5 6 7 8—04 03 02 01 00 99

Printed in the USA

CONTENTS

DAY 1

Job 1:1

There was a man in the land of Uz, whose name was Job; and that man was blameless and upright, and one who feared God and shunned evil.

Address Unknown

Someone once suggested that when many Christians flee from evil, they leave a forwarding address. They may not want to be immersed in sin, but they do want to stay in touch.

Job, on the other hand, was blameless and upright. How could he maintain such a spotless reputation? Because he did more than fear God; he also shunned evil. The word translated "shunned" can mean "to rebel" or "to revolt." You could say that Job found sin revolting. It was certainly not because he couldn't afford all the pleasures that lead to sin; Job was one of the wealthiest men of his time (Job 1:3). Nor did he live in some backwater village. The land of Uz was highly populated and had several kings or "sheiks" (Jer. 25:20). But Job had an attitude toward sin that left it no chance to get a toehold in his life. This man didn't simply avoid sin; he ran from it. And he gave no opportunity for it to contact him later.

It's not enough for Christians to avoid the sins they find attractive but stay in the vicinity where they can be found. Under those circumstances, you can be sure that you and your sin ultimately will get back together again. The only wise solution for those who want to live blameless and upright lives is to separate themselves far enough from enticing sin that no contact can take place.

If you've put a sin behind you, put everything associated with that sin behind you as well. If it's pornography, don't simply store your magazines out in the garage. Destroy them. If it's alcohol, don't leave a bottle in the house. Pour it down the drain. If it's gossip, cut your "grapevine." Don't attend those functions that degenerate into gossip sessions. You can do more than just refuse to participate; you can put some space between you and your temptation.

Flee sin and burn the bridges
behind you.

Reflections/Prayer Requests

_____

_____

_____

_____

_____

_____

_____

DAY 2

Job 1:5

So it was, when the days of feasting had run their course, that Job would send and sanctify them, and he would rise early in the morning and offer burnt offerings according to the number of them all. For Job said, "It may be that my sons have sinned and cursed God in their hearts." Thus Job did regularly.

A Family Man

In her book *Formations*, Kay Shurden observes that a family is more than a collection of human beings related by blood. It is more than the sum of its parts. A family is a living, shaping, powerful unit that teaches us our most important lessons. It teaches us who we are, how to act, whom we relate to and what is important in life.

Job was a busy man. He was a man of great wealth and responsibility. But his first priority, after his personal relationship with God, was his family. He rose "early in the morning" and brought his children before the Lord. He demonstrated his love for his family not only by providing for their physical well-being but also by interceding for them at God's throne of grace. Job modeled for his family the importance of a spiritual life and how to maintain that relationship with the Lord. And he did it on a regular basis.

Our lives are filled with stress and strain. The pressure to provide for the physical needs of our family is great. Yet to fulfill our complete responsibility to our loved ones, it is absolutely essential that we model an outstanding spiritual life as well. Without a role model to point the way, our children are at risk to falter in their personal walk with the Lord.

Are you providing more than a roof over your family's head and clothes on their back? These are vital, of course, but if you take your family responsibilities seriously, your spiritual responsibilities also will be important to you. Daily pray for each member of your family. Pay specific attention to their spiritual needs. Be a spiritual giant in their life. Provide for their spirit as diligently as you provide for their body.

Filling the soul is no less important than filling the stomach.

Reflections/Prayer Requests

_____

_____

_____

_____

_____

_____

DAY 3

Job 1:9–10

So Satan answered the LORD and said, "Does Job fear God for nothing? Have You not made a hedge around him, around his household, and around all that he has on every side? You have blessed the work of his hands, and his possessions have increased in the land."

God's Hedge

Some years ago a group of educators decided to remove the chain-link fence from around their school's playground. They believed the fence promoted feelings of confinement and restraint. But then a curious thing happened. They noticed that as soon as the fence was removed, the children huddled in the center of the playground to play. Unknown to the "experts," the children had actually gained a sense of security from the presence of the fence.

It was this same kind of security that Satan recognized in the life of Job. Figuratively speaking, God had placed a hedge or fence around Job and all he possessed to protect him from evil. Job was hemmed in on all sides by this hedge, but it was not a matter of constraint; it was a matter of security. He could live confidently, knowing that nothing could reach him without first going through God's hedge of protection.

Every believer today can have that same assurance. The Bible provides a first line of defense. The commandments and exhortations that some people view as divine restrictions are really God's protection plans. Their purpose is to prevent us from engaging in behavior that will hurt us. In addition, even the omnipotent hands of God are encircling our lives. No disaster or calamity can touch us without the permissive will of our Heavenly Father. Only those things that God knows ultimately will prove to be for our good are allowed to penetrate this divine hedge.

So, do not chafe against the restrictions God puts into your life. They are hedges for your security. Rejoice that God has His arms underneath you (Deut. 33:27) and His hands behind, before and over you (Ps. 139:5). You are totally encompassed by His hedge of protection. Inside God's hedge you are safe!

God's hedges are built for protection, not imprisonment.

Reflections/Prayer Requests

_____

_____

_____

_____

_____

DAY 4

Job 1:11–12

"But now, stretch out Your hand and touch all that he has, and he will surely curse You to Your face!" So the LORD said to Satan, "Behold, all that he has is in your power; only do not lay a hand on his person." So Satan went out from the presence of the LORD.

Lion on a Leash

Many cities and even small towns have leash laws. You can't simply let your pets run loose; they must be kept on a leash. The logic is obvious. With no constraints, dogs and cats not only do unsightly things on people's yards, but they damage shrubs and flowers, dig holes in unwanted places or make a nuisance of themselves in other ways.

God also has a leash law, and the primary target of that law is Satan. The Devil is a powerful enemy and can cause you a great deal of damage. The apostle Peter compared him to a lion (1 Pet. 5:8). Yet the life of Job demonstrates that the Devil can only go as far as God's leash allows him. With God's permission, Satan could afflict God's servant only to a certain extent and no further. Even though tragic events took place, God's hand was always on the leash preventing Satan from destroying Job.

Sometimes when we look at our difficult situations, we become fearful. Our imagination provides fertile soil for us to grow all kinds of potential problems and disasters. We fear the worst and are sure that we will be overwhelmed. Yet God never removes His hand from our enemy's leash. While we may experience difficult people and hard times, Satan cannot attack us beyond the limit that God allows.

Trust your Heavenly Father's wisdom. Nobody knows better than He does how far to play out the leash. While Satan may appear as a fearsome lion, he can do no more in your life than what God allows him. On that you can rely.

You can't trust the lion, but you can trust God's leash.

Reflections/Prayer Requests

_____

_____

_____

_____

_____

_____

_____

_____

_____

_____

DAY 5

Job 1:20

*Then Job arose and tore his robe
and shaved his head, and he fell to the
ground and worshiped.*

Rubble Reaction

A Sunday school teacher was giving an object lesson on reactions. She placed a glass on a small table and carefully filled it to the brim with water. Then she gave the table a slight shake and some of the water sloshed out. "Oh, my," she said, "I spilled some grape juice." A hand shot up. "But that's water," said a little boy. "That's right," she replied. "That's like our reactions. We might want to react a certain way to the things that shake our lives, but only what we've put in can come out."

Job's life was severely shaken. He first lost his wealth and his servants (Job 1:14–17). If that were not enough, he then lost his children (vv. 18–19). He later lost his health (2:7–8) and, finally, even his wife seemed to turn against him (v. 9). This series of blows caused two reactions to spill out of him. One was grief. He tore his robe and shaved his head. But the other was total submission to God. He fell to the ground and worshiped. It was obvious that what filled him most was love for and trust in the God of heaven.

Life is full of events that shake us. What spills out of us depends on what we've put in us. If you've been prone to harbor grudges and bitterness, you can guess what will gush out—anger and hatred. If you've sought to be filled with the Holy Spirit and the things of God, that also will be obvious by your reactions. No matter how you might wish otherwise, only those things that are in you can spill out.

If your life were reduced to a rubble heap and all that you hold dear were gone, how would you respond? Seek now to fill yourself with God's peace and love so you won't be ashamed at what comes spilling out of your life in hard times.

What we put in our lives will surely one day come out.

Reflections/Prayer Requests

_____

_____

_____

_____

_____

_____

_____

_____

_____

DAY 6

Job 1:21

And he said: "Naked I came from my mother's womb, and naked shall I return there. The LORD gave, and the LORD has taken away; blessed be the name of the LORD."

You Can't Take It with You

A few years ago, advice columnist Ann Landers printed a supposedly true story of a tightfisted husband who was married to a gracious woman. The wife put up with his tightwad behavior for more than 40 years. At age 60, "Ollie" was stricken with cancer. Toward the end, he made his wife promise, in front of witnesses, that she would place in his coffin all the money he had stashed away so he could buy his way into heaven. She agreed and assured him, as a woman of her word, she would do as he asked. The morning after his death she took the money (about $26,000) and deposited it in the bank. She then wrote a check and put it in the casket four days later. She knew he couldn't take it with him.

Job, however, never entertained the foolish ideas of the tightfisted husband. He realized that he would leave this world as naked as he entered. He was wise enough to know that he would take nothing away from this world but himself.

What we make of ourselves in terms of character rather than possessions should be our concern as Christians. A godly nature steeped in an understanding of God's Word and God's ways is far more valuable than earthly wealth or honors. When we stand before the Judgment Seat of Christ, what we are will be of greater importance than what we had (2 Cor. 5:10).

Begin now to cultivate those things that will not be left behind when your body is placed in the ground. Set aside some time each day to spend in the Bible and prayer. Develop an attitude of compassion and generosity. Allow God's Spirit to create in you a clean heart and a steadfast spirit. These are riches you can take with you.

You have to leave the world naked, but not destitute.

Reflections/Prayer Requests

_____

_____

_____

_____

_____

_____

_____

_____

DAY 7

Job 2:9

*Then his wife said to him, "Do you still hold
fast to your integrity? Curse God and die!"*

Don't Give Up and Don't Give In

Some of Andrew Jackson's boyhood
friends just couldn't understand how he
became a famous general and then the
president of the United States. They knew
of other men who had greater talent but
who never made it as far as Andrew did.
One of Jackson's friends said, "Why, Jim
Brown, who lived right down the road
from Jackson, was not only smarter but he
could throw Andy three times out of four
in a wrestling match." Another friend re-
sponded, "How did there happen to be a
fourth time? Didn't they usually say three
times and out?" "Sure, they were sup-
posed to," the man replied, "but not Andy.
He would never admit he was beat. Jim finally would get tired, and on the fourth try,
Andy would throw him and be the winner.
He just wouldn't quit."

No one could argue that Job's life was-
n't filled with severe trials. He not only
suffered the physical affliction of painful
boils from head to foot but also lost his
wealth and children. Then, to add insult to
injury, his wife urged him to give up. In her
estimation, life wasn't worth living. It was

time to curse God and die. Though Job didn't understand why he was being afflicted, however, he did know he wasn't willing to quit.

People are always ready to encourage you to give up. "Life is too difficult," they say. "Life is not fair. It hurts too much." But such advice fails to take into account the omnipotent hand of God. Even though we may not understand why painful and discouraging events happen in our lives, we have the assurance that God has His reasons—good reasons.

Don't allow anyone to talk you into quitting. Even though your trials may throw you for a loss time after time, you can have the confidence that God is still in control. Don't quit. Trust Him and keep on going. A day is coming when you'll be glad you did.

When you give up on yourself, you give up on God.

Reflections/Prayer Requests

_____

_____

_____

_____

_____

_____

DAY 8

Job 2:10

*But he said to her, "You speak as one
of the foolish women speaks. Shall we
indeed accept good from God, and shall
we not accept adversity?" In all this Job
did not sin with his lips.*

Keeping Your Balance

An old Arab proverb says, "All sun and
no rain makes a desert." Even nature
demonstrates the importance of dark
clouds and wet days. Without them, life
not only fails to grow but totally dries up
and blows away. Nothing but sunshine
would make for a barren and uninhabit-
able landscape.

Job realized this truth applied not only
to nature but to human life as well. It
would be foolish to think that God should
send only those things that appear to be
good without balancing them with those
experiences that appear to be bad. To accept the one and refuse the other is to
question God's wisdom. As painful as it
was to go through the loss of his possessions, his health and, most of all, his children, Job was unwilling to fault God. He
knew it was part of God's balance in life.

If given the option, most of us would
probably choose sunshine over rain, ice
cream over liver and joy over sadness.

Fortunately, God doesn't always give us a choice when it comes to things that challenge our lives. Both sorrow and gladness often come from sources over which we have no control. We can resist the trials and plead for only the "good" things, but this would be foolish. Without the balance between positives and negatives, our spiritual lives would be like the desert. The alternative is to submit to God and accept what He sends our way as part of His ultimate plan for our good.

You may not find it natural, but give thanks for the painful events that have happened in your life. Recognize them for what they are—a gift from the hand of the God who loves you. Acknowledge the truth that you need the rain as well as the sun to make your life complete. God gives you what is best for you. Trust Him and rejoice.

Without the rain, it's hard to fully appreciate the sunshine.

Reflections/Prayer Requests

_____

_____

_____

_____

_____

_____

DAY 9

Job 2:11, 13

*Now when Job's three friends heard of all
this adversity that had come upon him,
each one came from his own place—Eliphaz
the Temanite, Bildad the Shuhite, and Zophar
the Naamathite. For they had made an
appointment together to come and mourn
with him, and to comfort him.*

*So they sat down with him on the ground
seven days and seven nights, and no one
spoke a word to him, for they saw that his
grief was very great.*

The Power of Silence

We are a chatty society. If we're not on
the phone, we're sending e-mails. Should
e-mail not be available, then we dispatch
a fax. In fact, we're so addicted to verbal
communication that many people can't
leave home without a cell phone or pager
in their pocket. Yet in times of sorrow,
often silence says the most.

When Job's three friends arrived, they
could tell that he was in deep grief. But
rather than immediately offer their condo-
lences, they sat with him on the ground
for a whole week without saying a word.
They restrained what must have been a
strong urge to offer advice and sugges-
tions and chose instead to express their
sympathy by silently bearing his suffering
with him.

In the presence of grief, words sometimes are a hindrance. Often we resort to speaking because we're uncomfortable with the silence rather than because we have something to say. Consequently, when trying to console a friend we often engage in empty clichés. People who have borne deep anguish, however, testify that it is the silent presence of those who care that brings the deepest comfort. It is not their words but their quietly sharing the load of sorrow that helps the bereaved bear up under suffering.

Don't be in a hurry to speak to those who are grieving. A hug or a squeeze on the arm may bring more comfort than a hundred words. Ask God's Spirit to make it clear to you when He has prepared your friend's heart to hear your words. Until then, let your comfort be expressed in silence and in prayer rather than words.

Less talk often means more comfort.

Reflections/Prayer Requests

_____

_____

_____

_____

_____

_____

DAY 10

Job 3:9–12

"May the stars of its morning be dark; may it look for light, but have none, and not see the dawning of the day; because it did not shut up the doors of my mother's womb, nor hide sorrow from my eyes. Why did I not die at birth? Why did I not perish when I came from the womb? Why did the knees receive me? Or why the breasts, that I should nurse?"

In the Depths of Discouragement

Some time ago the Hayden Planetarium in New York City issued an invitation to all those interested in applying to join the crew on the first journey to another planet. Eighteen thousand people applied. They gave the applications to a panel of psychologists, who examined them thoroughly and came to this conclusion—in the vast majority of cases, those who applied did so because they were discouraged with their lives here and hoped they could find a new life somewhere else.

Job was mired even deeper in discouragement. He wasn't simply seeking a new life; he wished he had never been born. After losing his wealth, his health and his family, Job felt it would have been better had he never seen the light of his first day. Before we move too quickly to criticize Job, most of us have to admit we've never experienced in a matter of minutes the kind of devastating blows that this man did. Job went from the highest heights to the lowest depths with hardly time to take a breath.

Christians are not immune to disasters and the discouragement that sometimes accompanies them. But as Job was to discover later, we do have an answer—God. The Lord Jesus told His disciples, "Let not your heart be troubled; you believe in God, believe also in Me" (John 14:1). When your heart is filled with discouragement, Jesus can fill it with His peace.

If you are discouraged today, running away and starting a new life is not the answer. Instead, completely place your situation in Christ's hands. Turn over every troubling thought to His care. And let the peace of God, which surpasses understanding, give you new hope.

Let the God of peace fill you with the peace of God.

Reflections/Prayer Requests

_____

_____

_____

_____

_____

_____

DAY 11

Job 5:6–7

*For affliction does not come from the dust,
nor does trouble spring from the ground;
yet man is born to trouble,
as the sparks fly upward.*

Snafu

Perhaps you have heard someone talk about a snafu. You probably realized that this meant something had gone wrong, but you may not know how the word became a part of our English language. In reality, *snafu* is the first letter of each word in the phrase, "Situation normal, all fouled up." In other words, when something goes wrong, why be surprised? It's only normal for things to get fouled up. A snafu is something that can be expected. It's just a part of life.

Job's circumstances, of course, predate the word *snafu* but not the idea behind it. Job's friend Eliphaz recognized that "trouble" and "man" have a natural affinity for one another. As sparks from a fire are drawn upward by the rising heat, so trouble seems naturally drawn to man. It reflects another adage of our time: "If something can go wrong, it will." No matter when or where you live, snafus are going to find you.

Christians are sometimes dismayed when things go wrong in their lives. After all, when we trusted Jesus as our Savior, our troubles were suppose to be over, right? Yet the truth is much different. Jesus said, "In the world you will have tribulation" (John 16:33). That's just a normal part of living. The apostle Peter even said, "Beloved, do not think it strange concerning the fiery trial which is to try you, as though some strange thing happened to you" (1 Pet. 4:12). Snafus are not strange or out of the ordinary, even for Christians.

Perhaps you are experiencing a snafu today. Something you planned is fouled up. Don't be surprised. Instead, turn to God. When your life goes contrary to your expectations, He is able to give you either the wisdom to deal with it or the grace to live with it. Trust Him.

When trouble draws close, draw close to God.

Reflections/Prayer Requests

_____

_____

_____

_____

_____

_____

_____

_____

DAY 12

Job 5:17

"Behold, happy is the man whom God corrects; therefore do not despise the chastening of the Almighty."

God's Chastening

Lou Holtz, former head football coach of the Fighting Irish of Notre Dame, is legendary in his adherence to discipline. In an interview with *The Saturday Evening Post* in 1989, he was quoted as saying, "When it comes to discipline here, we ask three questions: Will it make him a better man? A better student? A better athlete? If the answer is yes, we make him do it. The next step is up to him. An individual has a choice when you discipline him: either to become bitter or better." Judging by his squad's record, both on and off the field, Lou Holtz's charges for the most part became better men.

Job's friends failed to understand God in many ways, but Eliphaz the Temanite was right in this respect. God's discipline is never meant to destroy but ultimately to bring joy. The word in this verse for "happy" (also translated "blessed") literally means "to walk straight." God's correction is given to keep His people from wandering away from the straight path and getting into situations that bring pain and heartache. Those who submit to His guidance will avoid many of the experiences that bring unhappiness to others.

God's discipline doesn't always feel good, especially if we fight against it. The writer of Hebrews confesses, "Now no chastening seems to be joyful for the present, but grievous" (12:11). Yet the writer continues, "Nevertheless, afterward it yields the peaceable fruit of righteousness to those who have been trained by it." A right relationship with God ultimately leads to a happiness that makes everything else seem insignificant.

Are you undergoing the chastening of God right now? If so, look ahead to the fruit He will bring out of this difficulty. Remember that God is seeking to correct your course so you can avoid future pitfalls that will bring you even greater pain. Let Him have His way in your life even if, at the moment, it's hard to bear. You'll be glad you did!

Pain now means gain later.

Reflections/Prayer Requests

DAY 13

Job 6:24–27

"Teach me, and I will hold my tongue; cause me to understand wherein I have erred. How forceful are right words! But what does your arguing prove? Do you intend to reprove my words, and the speeches of a desperate one, which are as wind? Yes, you overwhelm the fatherless, and you undermine your friend."

The Power of Words

In regions of South America there is a snake called the "two-step." If it bites you, you take two steps and die. Its venom swiftly paralyzes your nervous system, which stops your heart. But even if you don't visit South America, you're in peril of something else that is just as deadly. Words have the potential to kill relationships, paralyze love, poison minds, destroy faith, stain purity and de-face reputations.

Job recognized the capability of words to destroy when he exclaimed to his friends, "How forceful are right words!" After bearing up under the onslaught of Eliphaz the Temanite (Job 4:1–5:27), he was brought to the point of frustration. Instead of helping, his well-meaning companion only served to undermine his friend with his words (v. 27).

It is no small matter when we open our mouths. When our words are right, they can be a powerful force for good. But when they are wrong, they work like a deadly venom. Instead of being helpful, they are destructive. Rather than building up our friends, our words can tear them down. Those who are weak and helpless (Job's reference to the "fatherless" refers to these kinds of people) can be blown away by what we say.

Be careful today how you speak to others. Consider your words before you say them. Especially in times of crisis, the right word can bring healing and encouragement, while the wrong word can destroy your relationship with another person. Be sensitive to God's Spirit. Seek His guidance before you express yourself. And ask God to set a guard over your mouth to keep you from saying the wrong thing (Ps. 141:3).

Words are like dynamite; don't let them blow up in your face.

Reflections/Prayer Requests

_____

_____

_____

_____

_____

_____

_____

DAY 14

Job 7:6

"My days are swifter than a weaver's shuttle."

Fast, Faster, Fastest

Men have always had a love affair with speed. The faster they can go—first with horses, then with cars and now with space shuttles—the happier they are. Speed has increased to the point where we have moved from measuring events by the calendar (years, months, weeks) to often measuring them in nanoseconds (one billionth of a second) to reflect how fast things are moving. And what's more, each increase in speed is usually greeted with enthusiasm.

But that was not the case with Job. He bemoaned a speed that most of us are not too thrilled about—the speed with which the days of our lives go by. The fastest object Job had to compare his life to was the shuttle used by a weaver to create a piece of cloth. A skilled weaver could sling the shuttle back and forth at eye-blurring speed. Job's lament was that his days seemed to be going by as quickly as the weaver's shuttle.

The longer we live, the faster our days do seem to go by. Even though 24 hours is still the same, the events of our lives begin to stack up quickly on the history side. At the same time, the future side gets shorter and shorter, and the events of life seem to come more rapidly. This should motivate us to make sure that we diligently invest our time more wisely. As the days speed by like a weaver's shuttle, make sure you accomplish each day what the Lord wants you to do.

If you are putting things off until "someday," stop procrastinating. Do them now. Someday will be here and gone before you know it. The days of your life are being played out as rapidly as the fast-moving weaver's shuttle. Someday the shuttle will be stilled. Don't be caught with work for the Lord left undone.

Make sure when the cloth of your life is finished that no threads are missing.

Reflections/Prayer Requests

_____

_____

_____

_____

_____

_____

_____

_____

DAY 15

Job 9:2

*"Truly I know it is so, but how can a man be
righteous before God?"*

Righteous before God

According to *Parade* magazine, the zoo
in Copenhagen, Denmark, has put a
human couple on display. Henrik Leh-
mann and Malene Botoft live in a see-
through cage in the primate display next
to the baboons and monkeys. Their habi-
tat has a living room with furniture, a
computer, a television and a stereo. The
kitchen and bedroom are part of the display. Only the bathroom is excluded from
public view. Unlike their neighbors, who
aren't allowed out, the two humans occa-
sionally leave their fishbowl existence to
shop and water the flowers on their porch
back at home. But for the most part, their
lives are on public display.

Job realized that every human being
lives under similar conditions when it
comes to God. Nothing that we say or
even think is hidden from divine scrutiny.
Therefore, it is no surprise that Job won-
dered, perhaps with a hint of hopeless-
ness, how it might be possible to be righteous in God's sight. With every sin and
failure noted, who could possibly stand
before God?

When we compare ourselves with other people, we might feel that we're not all that bad. After all, we don't get drunk, use drugs or cheat on our income taxes. And when it comes to volunteering for charity, helping at church or just spending time with our family, we may even be sterling examples. But take one look at God's standards and you'll see a different picture. As He looks into our hearts to see our motives and view our hidden thoughts, our self-imposed halo begins to slip. It becomes obvious that Job's question needs to become our own: How can I be righteous before God?

If you are sensing your own need for a right relationship with God, be assured that He has provided a way. Through His Son, Jesus Christ, all your sins have been paid for and you can be forgiven. When you receive Him as your Savior, you stand in His righteousness before the Father. Trust Jesus today and live right before God in the righteousness of His Son.

Christ's righteousness makes us right with God.

Reflections/Prayer Requests

_____

_____

_____

DAY 16

Job 11:7

*"Can you search out the deep things of God?
Can you find out the limits of the Almighty?"*

A Big God

As the people of Job's day walked the earth, they likely didn't know that our world is 8,000 miles in diameter, with approximately 198,980,000 square miles on its surface. It is unlikely that they realized that this globe we call home is composed of 264 billion cubic miles. Most surely it was beyond their knowledge to compute that even though Earth is big, Saturn is 995 times bigger and Jupiter is 1,281 times bigger still. Furthermore, they had no inkling that beyond the few stars they could see there were at least 300 billion more.

Yet even without the benefit of all these mind-boggling figures, the people of Job's day knew that God, the Creator of all they saw, was bigger than anything they could comprehend. Zophar the Naamathite, one of Job's friends, was right when he said that no one could plumb God's depths or find God's limits. His thoughts run deeper than any human wisdom; His power outstrips man's best efforts.

Some people object to the concept of God because He is beyond their ability to understand. They argue that if they can't comprehend Him, then certainly He must not exist. Others simply dismiss Him as irrelevant because He fails to act as they feel He should. Yet God says, "For as the heavens are higher than the earth, so are My ways higher than your ways, and My thoughts than your thoughts" (Isa. 55:9). Who is man to try to whittle God down to what he can understand?

Let God be God. Don't try to shrink Him down to fit neatly within your scheme of things. If He were small enough for you to comprehend, He wouldn't be big enough for you to worship. The fact that He is beyond your understanding is confirmation that no situation will ever exceed His ability to handle it. To live confidently, you don't have to understand God—you just have to trust Him.

***Only small people insist
on a small God.***

Reflections/Prayer Requests

_____

_____

_____

_____

_____

_____

DAY 17

Job 13:15

"Though He slay me, yet will I trust Him."

Total Trust

Years ago a military officer and his wife were aboard a ship that was caught in a raging storm at sea. Seeing his wife's fear, the man tried to comfort her. Suddenly she grasped his sleeve and cried, "How can you be so calm?" He stepped back and drew his sword. Pointing it at her, he asked, "Are you afraid of this?" "Of course not!" she answered. "Why not?" he inquired. "Because I know you love me too much to hurt me," she said. He replied, "I also know the One who holds the winds and the waters in the hollow of His hand, and He loves us too much to fail to care for us!"

Job had that same trust. He had lost his children, his wealth and his health. Even his wife had turned against him. He had only one more thing to lose—his own life. Yet Job declared that even if it were to come down to that final loss, he would continue to trust that God had a purpose in everything that happened to him. In Job's eyes, the important issue was not what was happening but whose hand was behind it. If God did it, Job knew he could trust it.

Often our trust is based on the "what" rather than the "who." We focus on the event rather than the One who controls that event. Consequently, when trials and tribulations come crashing down upon us, our faith is shaken. We can't understand why a loving Heavenly Father would allow such grief to enter our lives. Yet if we truly believe that He is loving, we can say with Job that even though He slay us, we will believe He intends it for our good. In His infinite wisdom and goodness, He will take the most difficult circumstances and use them for our good.

When you are facing life's most severe trials, focus on the character of God. Build your trust on who God is, not on what is taking place. When you know who He is, you never have to worry about what He will allow to happen.

Trust is based on character, not circumstances.

Reflections/Prayer Requests

_____

_____

_____

_____

_____

_____

DAY 18

Job 14:14

*"If a man dies, shall he live again?
All the days of my hard service I will wait,
till my change comes."*

To Live Again

The Romanian weekly *Tinerama* reported that a woman fainted when she opened her front door and found her husband standing there. It all started when a man named Neagu choked on a fish bone, stopped breathing and collapsed. The family doctor, knowing Neagu's heart condition, didn't think twice about proclaiming the 71-year-old dead of a heart attack. But three days later, grave diggers at the cemetery heard a suspicious sound. They opened Neagu's coffin to find him surrounded by wilted flowers but very much alive. It took Neagu three weeks to convince the authorities to cancel his death certificate from their register.

Job, however, had more in mind than mere resuscitation. As he looked ahead to that day when he would put aside his mortal body, he asked the age-old question, "Will I live again?" Implied in Job's question is not the hopeless uncertainty of the pagan world but a quiet confidence that someday it would be so. As a result, he was willing to plod through his trials patiently, knowing that a greater and more glorious day lay ahead.

As believers in Christ, we have even more reason to be confident. We have not only the promise of resurrection (1 Cor. 6:14) but also the example of Christ (Luke 24:1–3). The apostle Paul assured us that what is sown perishable shall be raised imperishable (1 Cor. 15:42–44). That which is placed in the ground will some-day be resurrected to rejoin the spirit from which it was separated and together spend eternity with the Lord (1 Thess. 4:14–17).

If you are troubled by pain and disap-pointment, be encouraged by what is to come. Wait patiently for that day when God will give you a new body in which to live a new life. The difficulties we experi-ence now will one day vanish into eter-nity. Take heart—the best is yet to be.

Real life begins after this life.

Reflections/Prayer Requests

_____

_____

_____

_____

_____

_____

DAY 19

Job 19:25

*For I know that my Redeemer lives,
and He shall stand at last on the earth.*

My Redeemer Lives

Some years ago an article appeared in *National Geographic* magazine that told of a young man from Hanover, Pennsylvania, who was badly burned in a boiler explosion. To save his life, physicians covered him with 6,000 square centimeters of donor skin as well as sheets of skin cultured from a stamp-sized piece of his own unburned skin. A journalist later asked him, "Do you ever think about the donor who saved you?" The young man replied, "To be alive because of someone else is too big, too much, so I don't think about it."

Job, on the other hand, not only thought about the One who would save him, he longed for Him. As he looked at his life, he realized his need for a redeemer. In spite of his best efforts, his life fell far short of the perfection that God required. Yet he rejoiced in the fact that the One who would pay the price for his sins was alive—not only alive, but would someday actually stand upon the earth. It was on this great event that Job pinned all his hopes.

For those of us who live on this side of Christ's birth, we know that our Redeemer came, lived among us and died on the cross for our sins. And, like Job, that is the great event on which we pin all our hopes. Even though it took place centuries ago, the death and resurrection of Jesus is the crux around which everything else revolves. Because of this Redeemer, we have the assurance that we are free from the penalty of sin. The price has been paid, God's justice has been satisfied, and we are restored to a full relationship with the Father.

Have you been redeemed? If not, Christ offers you that opportunity right now. He paid the price for your sins when He died in your place at Calvary's cross. Accept Him as your Redeemer today. If you've done that, then give Him thanks. Christ has set you free.

Redemption: don't leave life without it.

Reflections/Prayer Requests

_____

_____

_____

_____

_____

DAY 20

Job 20:4–5

*"Do you not know this of old, since man
was placed on earth, that the triumphing
of the wicked is short, and the joy
of the hypocrite is but for a moment?"*

Momentary Pleasures

John Bunyan was a Puritan preacher
and author of the classic *Pilgrim's
Progress*. A local magistrate threatened to
put Bunyan in prison unless he promised
that he would not preach, but he refused
to quit. For the next 12 years (1660-1672),
he was intermittently in and out of jail.
Defiantly he declared that he would remain in prison until the moss grew on his
eyelids rather than fail to do what God had
commanded him to do. To John Bunyan,
the pleasures that come with freedom
were not worth the price of disobedience.

Job's friend Zophar the Naamathite understood this as well. He was wrong in as-
suming Job had some hidden sin in his life
that he would not confess. Zophar was
right, however, in pointing out that the
pleasures enjoyed by the wicked and the
hypocrites are only momentary. As sub-
stantial as they might seem, perhaps con-
tinuing for many years, compared with the
rewards of the righteous that will last for
eternity, such pleasures are short-lived.

Stripped of sin's glamour, it's obvious that the ungodly are making a pretty poor deal.

We should always make choices with God's timetable in mind. While the pleasures available to those willing to compromise their stand for the Lord are varied and enticing, they can endure at best for only a lifetime. On the other hand, the psalmist reminds us, "At Your right hand are pleasures forevermore" (Ps. 16:11). How shortsighted it would be to choose a few years of comfort and ease over the never-ending pleasures that God has stored up for those who are faithful to Him.

If you are facing a choice today, ask yourself if your decision will result in temporary pleasures or eternal rewards. That answer will make it clear which way you should go. If you live for what is eternal, the temporary will have little appeal.

Today is no substitute for eternity.

Reflections/Prayer Requests

_____

_____

_____

_____

_____

_____

DAY 21

Job 23:10

"But He knows the way that I take; when He has tested me, I shall come forth as gold."

Like Gold

It's a well-known fact that many people have become successful by compensating for personality or physical flaws. Winston Churchill, for example, stuttered as a youth yet became a great orator. Glenn Cunningham was so badly burned as a boy it was thought he would never walk again. He became, however, one of the world's great milers. George Bernard Shaw was so painfully shy that he found it difficult to talk with anyone. But Shaw forced himself to join organizations where he would have to speak before audiences. In each of these situations, it was the fiery trials that brought out the best in the person.

As Job looked at the tests that God allowed in his life, he did not despair. Instead, he saw them as the instruments that would be used to bring about good. He knew that as the heat of a fiery furnace was needed to remove the dross from precious metal, so it took the cleansing flames of affliction to remove thoroughly the impurities from his life. He was confident that he would come forth not as a burned-up cinder but as a nugget of purest gold.

God is not in the demolition business, but He does run a refinery. His purpose is not to destroy but to purify. The burning difficulties that test us are designed to remove the dregs that hinder us from serving Him with clean hands and a pure heart. He seeks not to ruin us but to increase our value. His desire is to separate from us anything that would detract from our worth and make us ever more useful in service to Him.

If you are in the fiery furnace of affliction, take heart. God's hand is on the thermostat. He will allow the heat to do no more than remove the impurities. As you go in mixed with the dregs of this world, you will come forth pure and refined.

Only precious ore is put in the Refiner's fire.

Reflections/Prayer Requests

_____

_____

_____

_____

_____

_____

_____

DAY 22

Job 28:12, 28

*"But where can wisdom be found?
And where is the place of understanding?"*

*And to man He said, "Behold, the fear of the
Lord, that is wisdom, and to depart from evil
is understanding."*

Where Is Wisdom?

A young man got into financial difficulty by loaning a friend in another town
$500. He neglected to ask his friend to sign
a written note. He didn't even ask for a re-
ceipt indicating the amount loaned. When
the young man needed his money back, he
realized he had nothing with which to
document his claim. In desperation he
turned to his father for advice. After a moment of consideration, the father said,
"Write him and say you need the $1,000
you loaned him." The young man said,
"You mean $500." "No," said the father,
"you say $1,000, and he will immediately
write back that he owes you only $500.
Then you will have it in writing." The son
followed his father's wisdom and the prob-
lem was solved.

Job, too, was perplexed by his situation.
He had been a righteous man, yet now it
seemed as though his world was falling
apart. He felt the need for wisdom. "But
where," he asked, "do I find it?" His Heavenly Father gave him the answer: It is in

the fear of (respect for) the Lord. Only to the degree that those who seek wisdom are willing to respect God will they be motivated to apply the truths that He shares with them.

If earthly fathers can give wise counsel, how much more so can our Heavenly Father? But to gain true benefit from that counsel we must have reverence toward the One who gives it. Unless we respect the source, we'll never value the product. We not only need to hear, but we also must heed.

If you are looking for wisdom today, the best source you'll ever find is as close to you as your Bible. God speaks clearly through His Word to give you the guidance you need for your daily life. If you fear Him, obey what He says and take note of the benefit of heeding His Word.

If you respect the Lord, you'll benefit from His wisdom.

Reflections/Prayer Requests

_____

_____

_____

_____

_____

_____

DAY 23

Job 31:1

"I have made a covenant with my eyes; why then should I look upon a young woman?"

The Eyes Have It

Millie Dienert worked with the Billy Graham evangelistic team for 40 years. She commented, "I have always appreciated from a moral point of view how the men have been in their attitude toward the secretaries. The doors are always left open. They have always kept everything above reproach. When you are working on a long-term basis with the same person, constantly in hotels where the wife is not there and the secretary is, that is a highly explosive situation. You have to take precautions. I have always respected the way they have handled that."

Job also desired to live a chaste life. Even though he was a married man, he knew how easy it would be to slip. And it all begins with a look. Perhaps at first it is nothing more than just a casual glance, but then comes a lingering stare. Before long the look becomes something more. Therefore, Job made a covenant with his eyes, where it all begins. He knew that if nothing was started, he wouldn't have to worry about where it would go.

Christians need to remember that immorality begins with the eyes. Where people look, how long they look and what they allow to be communicated through their eyes are all factors that can bring about a fall. What we allow to come in through the eye-gate makes or breaks our Christian testimony. If we set up a roadblock at the source of our temptation, we can insure that our witness for the Lord will remain untainted.

Begin with the eyes. You can't help the first look, but you are definitely responsible for every look thereafter. Close that gate as soon as you can. Make a covenant with yourself and the Lord that you will not allow your eyes to be your downfall. Guard your eyes, and the rest of your behavior will be easier to control.

Wrong looks lead to wrong behavior.

Reflections/Prayer Requests

_____

_____

_____

_____

_____

_____

_____

_____

_____

DAY 24

Job 31:24–25, 28

"If I have made gold my hope, or said to fine gold, 'You are my confidence'; if I have rejoiced because my wealth was great, and because my hand had gained much; . . . this also would be an iniquity worthy of judgment, for I would have denied God who is above."

Trusting in Your Treasures

Dr. Howard Hendricks, a professor at Dallas Theological Seminary, shared how he and his wife, Jeanne, dined with a very rich man from a blue-blooded Boston family. During the course of the dinner, Dr. Hendricks asked him, "How in the world did you grow up in the midst of such wealth and not be consumed by materialism?" The man replied, "My parents taught us that everything in our home was either an idol or a tool."

Before the Sabeans raided his oxen and donkeys, the Chaldeans stole his camels and fire from heaven burned up his sheep, Job had been a very wealthy man, but he was also wise enough to know that these were not the things in which he should place his trust. In fact, had he done so, he would have been worthy of all the affliction he experienced. It would have made him guilty of denying God the most important place in his life.

Wealth is not wrong, but how we view our possessions can be very wrong. Christians must realize that everything we have is a gift from the Lord. When what we have received becomes more important than the One who gave it, we have fallen into the trap of idolatry. We are putting possessions ahead of the Lord. Our security then rests not in whom we belong to but in what belongs to us.

You may not consider yourself wealthy. Most people don't. But whether you have a lot or a little, your attitude toward what you do possess may be causing you to stumble. Examine your heart. Are your possessions a tool to be used for God's glory or an idol in which you trust?

Honor the Giver more than the gift.

Reflections/Prayer Requests

_____

_____

_____

_____

_____

_____

_____

_____

DAY 25

Job 32:9

*"Great men are not always wise, nor do
the aged always understand justice."*

No Guarantees

When we buy a product, especially an expensive item such as an automobile or a computer, we want to know what guarantees come with it. What does the company that made the item promise to do for the one who bought it? If it ceases to function six months after we purchase it, will the manufacturer guarantee to replace it at no cost to the buyer? What if we're simply not satisfied with the way it works? Can it be returned? Next to the price, the guarantees that come with a product can be the most influential selling point.

The fourth friend of Job, Elihu, the son of Barachel the Buzite, made a valid observation. The youngest of those seeking to help Job during his time of trouble, he declared that there are no guarantees in life. As he considered the advice given by his more esteemed colleagues, it was obvious to him that they were off base. He realized that their reputed greatness didn't guarantee their wisdom, nor did the fact that they were older than he mean that they understood justice. Nothing about life is guaranteed.

Yet for those who have placed their faith in Christ, life is not that gloomy. It is still true that following certain practices will not guarantee a particular result. Godly parents have raised prodigal children. Committed Christians have contracted incurable diseases. Devout believers have lost all their possessions. But God does make this guarantee—eventually everything will turn out all right. He promises, "All things work together for good to those who love God, to those who are the called according to His purpose" (Rom. 8:28). That's the best guarantee of all.

Face it—you have no guarantees in life. But God is able to massage your life and make it fit into His guarantee. Whatever happens to you, God guarantees He will use it for your good.

What life lacks, God supplies.

Reflections/Prayer Requests

_____

_____

_____

_____

_____

_____

_____

DAY 26

Job 34:10

*"Therefore listen to me, you men
of understanding: Far be it from God
to do wickedness, and from the Almighty
to commit iniquity."*

Don't Blame God

A man was handing out business cards that read, "Federman and Coe, Merchants." When asked about his partner the man admitted there was no such person. "Then why do you have the name on your card?" someone wanted to know. "Well, you see," the man replied, "if something goes wrong I just blame it on Coe. That way I get out of trouble easily."

Three of Job's friends were suggesting the same. As they saw it, God was responsible for all the evil that had befallen Job. Even though they suspected some hidden sin in Job's life, his troubles still came down to a smear on God's character. But Elihu, Job's fourth friend, objected to such a charge. God does not commit wickedness, even if some might consider it justified. Admittedly, we have the benefit of seeing behind the scenes and knowing that it was Satan who committed these acts of iniquity. But Eliphaz, Bildad and Zophar could have realized the same if they had truly understood God's nature.

Christians are good at blaming God when things go wrong. If a child dies, it's God's fault. If the house burns down, it's God's fault. Such accusations cannot be true. God permits bad things to happen, but He doesn't cause them. Sometimes things happen because of our own carelessness or sinfulness. Other times they happen because of the forces of evil in the world. But God is not to blame. James says, "Every good gift and every perfect gift is from above, and comes down from the Father of lights, with whom there is no variation or shadow of turning" (James 1:17). We may not understand much about God, but there is one thing we can know for certain: There is no "dark side" to God.

Don't blame the Lord for your troubles. They come as a result of sin in this world. Confess to God any anger or bitterness you might feel for what you've experienced in life. Then ask Jesus to heal your wounds and make you whole.

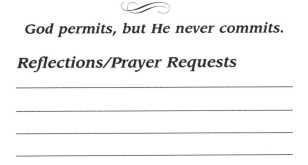

God permits, but He never commits.

Reflections/Prayer Requests

_____

_____

_____

_____

_____

DAY 27

Job 34:21–22

"For His eyes are on the ways of man, and He sees all his steps. There is no darkness nor shadow of death where the workers of iniquity may hide themselves."

No Place to Hide

Have you noticed that when people try to hide from trouble they rarely succeed? A true story relates that a retired couple was alarmed by the threat of nuclear war, so they undertook a serious study of all the inhabited places on the globe. Their goal was to determine what geographical location would be least likely affected by a nuclear war. They studied books and traveled the world and finally found the place. That Christmas they sent their pastor a card from their new home on the Falkland Islands. Shortly afterwards, however, their "paradise" was turned into a war zone by Great Britain and Argentina. Even though they had tried to hide from trouble, trouble had found them.

Elihu, Job's youngest friend, made this same observation about God. No one can hide from Him. His all-seeing eyes observe man's every step. Although Elihu was wrong in his assumption that Job had some hidden sin in his life, he was right to claim that nothing could be concealed from God's sight. Had Job truly been a worker of iniquity, God would have known it.

Sometimes we feel frustrated because many evildoers are able to cover their wickedness so cleverly that they never can be brought to trial. Other times they simply disappear with their ill-gotten gains and no one can find them. But no one escapes the watchful eye of God. He knows what they've done and where they can be found. When the time is right, God will make sure justice is done.

If you are the victim of a miscarriage of justice or know some guilty person who has disguised his wrongdoing, be encouraged. No one can hide from the Lord. The most clever criminal can never conceal his deeds or himself from the watchful eyes of God. God observes all that we do, and He is a just Judge.

Justice is blind, but God isn't.

Reflections/Prayer Requests

_____

_____

_____

_____

_____

_____

_____

DAY 28

Job 37:23–24

"As for the Almighty, we cannot find Him; He is excellent in power, in judgment and abundant justice; He does not oppress. Therefore men fear Him; He shows no partiality to any who are wise of heart."

No Partiality

Gandhi says in his autobiography that in his student days he was truly interested in the Bible. Deeply touched by reading the Gospels, he seriously considered becoming a convert, since Christianity seemed to offer the real solution to the caste system that was dividing the people of India. One Sunday he went to a nearby church. He decided to see the minister and ask for instruction in the way of salvation and enlightenment on other doctrines. But when he entered the sanctuary, the ushers refused to give him a seat and suggested that he go worship with his own people. Gandhi left and never came back. *If Christians have caste differences also*, he said to himself, *I might as well remain a Hindu*. The partiality showed by those Christians had a devastating effect on India and the world.

Elihu implied that Job may have set himself apart as something special because of his wealth, perhaps even thinking he could buy his way out of affliction

(Job 36:18–19). While this was not a correct assessment of Job's character, Elihu made a valid point: God shows no partiality. God doesn't care about a person's wealth, social status or skin color, but only about his heart. God accepts all those who are "wise in heart."

Christians have fallen into the trap of partiality almost from the beginning. James warned his readers about showing favoritism to the wealthy (James 2:1–4). Other Christians have shown partiality based on language, nationality or ethnicity. None of these things, however, are important to God. He looks beneath such surface issues and considers what a person is on the inside.

If you find yourself hung up on a person's economic status or skin color, ask God to help you see past these superficial matters. Seek to know others as God does—by their heart.

Have no part in partiality.

Reflections/Prayer Requests

_____

_____

_____

_____

_____

_____

DAY 29

Job 38:1

*Then the Lord answered Job
out of the whirlwind.*

Out of the Whirlwind

Violent storms are one of the most destructive forces that nature can unleash upon mankind. Living in Nebraska, I've noticed that there is rarely a spring night during which some part of the state isn't pounded by tornadoes or torrential rainfalls. Unfortunately, these outbreaks of nature are usually accompanied by a great deal of property damage, sometimes even loss of life. Whirlwinds are definitely forces to be reckoned with.

But the whirlwind that Job encountered was more than a product of nature. It was a divine messenger from the Lord. God used one of nature's most awesome expressions of power to confront Job with his own frailty and weakness. The whirlwind brought Job face to face with his lack of understanding of God. Obviously his friends had misunderstood the nature of God as well, but Job was not entirely innocent either. After he experienced the violence of this whirling windstorm, he was brought to a fresh realization that God was far greater than he could comprehend. With his ignorance revealed, Job confessed, "I have uttered what I did not understand, things too wonderful for me, which I did not know" (Job 42:3).

In the midst of our distress, it is common to find fault with God. We think, *Surely God must have made a mistake for this to be happening to me.* But such thinking is foolishness. With our limited understanding of what is truly happening both on earth and in heaven, we are arrogant to think that we are in a position to judge God's actions. We are dealing with issues that are far beyond our understanding. In fact, even if God were to explain them, we wouldn't be able to fully grasp them.

God is not committed to give you answers, but He is committed to bring you comfort. Avail yourself of what God offers—His presence in the midst of tribulation—and leave the rest up to someone far wiser than yourself.

Answers don't always comfort, but God does.

Reflections/Prayer Requests

_____

_____

_____

_____

_____

_____

_____

DAY 30

Job 42:5–6

"I have heard of You by the hearing of the ear, but now my eye sees You. Therefore I abhor myself, and repent in dust and ashes."

Seeing Is Believing

All of his life, John Wesley had been very pious. He got up at 4 A.M. and prayed for two hours. He would then read the Bible for an hour before going to the jails and hospitals to minister to all kinds of people. He would teach, pray for and help others until late at night. A turning point for Wesley came, however, when he found his way to a chapel on Aldersgate Street in London. He heard a man reading a sermon that described a personal relationship with Jesus Christ. Wesley suddenly realized that he was trusting his good works. That night he wrote in his journal: "About a quarter before nine, while he described the change which God works in the heart through faith in Christ, I felt my heart strangely warmed. I felt I did trust in Christ, Christ alone, for salvation; and an assurance was given me that He had taken away my sins, even mine, and saved me from the law of sin and death."

Job also had been a pious man. Even God pointed him out as an extraordinarily righteous individual. But apparently something was lacking. He had heard about God and had been obedient to the degree that he knew how. But when he met God in the whirlwind, a new dimension was added to his life. God was no longer simply what he had heard about; He was now someone Job had personally experienced.

Those who grow up in the church often spend their early years hearing about God. Based on what they hear, they may lead a moral life and feel they know Jesus Christ. Yet they have had no personal encounter with Him. He is the God of their heads but not their hearts.

Make sure that your faith is not based merely on what you've heard. Seek a personal encounter with Jesus Christ through His Word. Allow God to become a real person in your life, not just someone you've heard about. Jesus came seeking you (Luke 19:10); now it's your turn to seek Him.

***Hearing is no substitute
for experiencing.***

Reflections/Prayer Requests

_____

_____

_____

_____

_____

DAY 31

Job 42:10

*And the L*ORD *restored Job's losses when he prayed for his friends. Indeed the L*ORD *gave Job twice as much as he had before.*

Boomerang Prayer

In my office in Lincoln, Nebraska, I have on my desk two boomerangs from Australia. One is the genuine article, the other is a tourist version, but they both do what boomerangs are suppose to do. If you hold them the right way and throw them with that special flick of the wrist, they will fly out from your hand, circle back around and return to you. With a boomerang, what you send out also comes back.

Job experienced the same thing with prayer. Job's three friends found themselves in deep trouble with God. The Lord said to Eliphaz the Temanite, "My wrath is aroused against you and your two friends, for you have not spoken of Me what is right" (Job 42:7). Having been on the receiving end of these misguided barbs, Job might have been tempted to rejoice that God was setting these men straight. But instead, at God's request, he prayed for them. And as he prayed for their forgiveness and restoration, God turned these prayers for blessing back onto Job and restored twice as much as Job had before.

When people have hurt and offended us, we often pray that God will help them see the error of their ways. And should God choose to extract a bit of vengeance, we wouldn't be opposed to that either. But the real joy comes if we can put our pain behind us and pray for God's blessing on them. Jesus says, "Do good to those who hate you, and pray for those who spitefully use you and persecute you" (Matt. 5:44). We are to pray for their good, not for their harm.

If you have been the object of someone's misunderstanding, pray for that person. Ask God to richly bless him. You will be surprised to find that the blessings may boomerang back to you as well.

***Praying for others is the best thing
we can do for ourselves.***

Reflections/Prayer Requests

_____

_____

_____

_____

_____

_____

_____

_____

_____

GIANTS OF THE OLD TESTAMENT

Look for these other titles in the series: